The Body in the Woods

BE A CRIME SCENE INVESTIGATOR

by Alix Wood

Gareth Stevens
PUBLISHING

Please visit our website, **www.garethstevens.com**. For a free color
catalog of all our high-quality books, call toll free 1-800-542-2595
or fax 1-877-542-2596

Cataloging-in-Publication Data

Names: Wood, Alix.
Title: The body in the woods: be a crime scene investigator / Alix Wood.
Description: New York : Gareth Stevens Publishing, 2018. | Series: Crime solvers | Includes index.
Identifiers: ISBN 9781538206355 (pbk.) | ISBN 9781538206294 (library bound) | ISBN 9781538206171 (6 pack)
Subjects: LCSH: Criminal investigation--Juvenile literature. | Crime scenes--Juvenile literature. | Crime scene
    searches--Juvenile literature.
Classification: LCC HV8073.8 W66 2018 | DDC 363.25--dc23

First Edition

Published in 2018 by
Gareth Stevens Publishing
111 East 14th Street, Suite 349
New York, NY 10003

Copyright © 2018 Alix Wood Books

Produced for Gareth Stevens by Alix Wood Books
Designed by Alix Wood
Editor: Eloise Macgregor
Consultant: Stacey Deville, MFS, Texas Forensic Investigative Consultants

Photo credits: Cover, 1, 3, 6, 7, 8, 10, 11, 12, 21, 22, 23, 25 top, 27, 28, 36, 38, 41, 43 © Adobe Stock Images, 4 © Harry
Graham, 9, 13, 14, 21 bottom, 25 bottom, 26 top, 29 top, 30, 32, 33, 39 © Alix Wood, 16 © 123RF, 20 © Shutterstock, 31
top © pixabay, 34 © iStock, all other images are in the public domain

Printed in the United States of America
CPSIA compliance information: Batch #CS17GS For further information contact Gareth Stevens, New York, New York at 1-800-542-2595.

CONTENTS

call the csi team...

One bright morning in October, local woman Annie Lewis is jogging along a trail through the woods. Out of the corner of her eye, she notices a large, rolled up blanket. Annie jogs here every day, so she knows it wasn't there yesterday. She goes over to take a look...

DISPATCHER: Emergency 911. What is the location of your emergency?

ANNIE: I'm at Tall Trees Trail, Saunderstone. Please come quickly. I'm scared.

DISPATCHER: What is your name, caller?

ANNIE: I'm Annie Lewis. I think I have just found a dead body!

DISPATCHER: What makes you think that, Annie?

ANNIE: I found a man, wrapped in a blanket...

Reporting Officer's Notes

6:30 am: Dispatch receives a 911 call. A dead body has been found at the Tall Trees Trail, Saunderstone. The caller identifies herself as Annie Lewis.

Unit 367 is dispatched and arrives at the scene at 6:37 am. The officers confirm that there is a body. They secure the scene. Emergency Medical Services confirm that the body is dead.

6:59 am: Detectives Tom Vallejo and Kofi Adoji arrive at the scene. The Crime Scene Investigator (CSI) team is called to the scene, too.

The body of an adult, white male is found partly hidden in bushes. The body is wrapped in a blue blanket. He is on his back. His left leg is bent at the knee, his arms raised near his head. He is wearing gray pants, a black sweater, and a blue checkered scarf. There is apparent blood on his chest.

Case File

The first officer on the scene starts to rope off the area, to protect vital **evidence**. Only essential people are allowed near the **crime scene** until the CSI team arrives. The detectives and the **coroner** enter to examine the body. They must be careful not to disturb any clues. Meanwhile, the officer scans the area. There is a chance the killer is still hiding nearby.

Solve It!

When the first officer on the scene fills out his report, which of these observations is the most important?

a) he hears birds singing

b) he hears a car engine

c) he hears the wind rustle the tree branches

Answers on page 45

meet a crime scene investigator

The call comes in to the CSI team. Andrea Bray grabs her equipment and heads for the door. After a long morning of **testifying** in court, she is already tired. It looks like this may turn out to be a very long day.

Andrea never knows what to expect when she is called to a crime scene. CSI teams go to many different types of crime scenes, such as burglaries, road traffic accidents, and sometimes, murders.

Solve It!

What do you think Andrea is doing in this picture?

a) she is keeping the evidence clean

b) she is dusting the cup to try to find any fingerprints

c) she is checking the cup for breakage

Answers on page 45

Name: Andrea Bray

Job: Crime Scene Investigator

Education: Studied for a degree in Chemistry

Previous jobs: Was a police officer for 5 years

Career:
Andrea has been a crime scene investigator for two years. She works for the Police Department.

Favorite school subject: Andrea always loved Science at school.

Favorite part of her job: Knowing that she has helped to solve a case.

Worst part of her job: There can be a lot of paperwork and report writing.

Most interesting case: Andrea once helped match tiny flecks of paint found on the body of a murder victim to a fretsaw found at the suspect's home. The paint from the saw was rare, so the match was enough to convince the jury of the suspect's guilt.

Skills of the trade

CSIs like Andrea must have a particular set of skills to do their job well. They need to be organized and patient. They must not be grossed out by some unpleasant sights, smells, and situations! CSIs need to pay attention to tiny details. The smallest scrap of evidence could be vitally important to the case. They also have to be good at recording what they find, and be able to stand up and present this information in a court of law.

Do you have what it takes?

You enter a room where a crime has been committed. What do you notice? You need to write down everything, even the smallest details. Can you smell anything? Is the window open? Is the heating or air-conditioning on? Which lights are on? Is the toilet seat up or down? All these tiny details need to be noted. They may not seem like much, but each could be a vital clue.

EVIDENCE BAG CHALLENGE

You will need: some brown paper bags, tweezers, latex or rubber gloves, a pen and paper

1 See if you can work out which person in your household used your kitchen last. First, check with your family that doing this is OK. Put on the gloves and search the room for evidence. Are there any dirty plates or cups? Can you tell what food was on them? Open the trash can and look in. What items were thrown away last? Does that give you a clue? Don't sift through all the trash, that could be pretty yucky!

2 Write down all the evidence. You may find that your evidence points to several people. Write their names down as suspects.

3 Interview your household and present your evidence. See who confesses!

CSIs need to be skilled photographers. Photographs are a great way to record the crime scene. Video can be useful, too. Usually Andrea will also sketch out a crime scene. She must be **methodical** in everything that she does. She must carefully check for and preserve evidence such as fingerprints, footprints, hair and fibers, and blood stains. Everything Andrea finds must be carefully recorded.

Recording the Crime Scene

Taking photographs of a crime scene helps detectives remember the position of everything. This detailed record may be vital to help solve the case once everything is cleared away. Look at the crime scene on page 11. What do you think you should photograph and videotape?

Recording

Photography Checklist

1. Take overall photos of the scene and overall area ☐
2. Take midrange photos of the evidence/body ☐
3. Take closeup photos of the evidence/body ☐
4. Use numbered tent markers to identify evidence ☐
5. Retake all photos listed in 1–3. ☐

40

EVIDENCE BAG CHALLENGE

Are pictures more accurate than notes? Try this challenge.

1 **You will need:** a pencil and paper

2 Cover up the picture at the bottom of this page.

3 Read Andrea's crime scene notes (right). Try to draw the scene using just her notes.

Uncover the picture and see how well you did.

The victim was on the gym floor. One arm and leg were raised. Possible blood surrounded the victim's head. Some spatters were on the wall. The window was broken. Two blue shoes were in the room, one under a weight bench and one on the shelf near the body. Another weight, on a mat, had possible blood under one end.

Top Tip

Andrea accurately says "possible blood" because it hasn't been proved that it is blood yet.

Andrea needs to add to her notes. They need to be more precise. Was broken glass inside or outside the room? Which wall were the red splatters on? Which end of the weight had the red stain? These details might be very important.

preserving the evidence

When Andrea and her team reach the crime scene, the area has already been taped off by a police officer. Andrea's team needs to make sure that they don't **contaminate** the area with their own hair or **fibers**. Andrea ties her long hair back. The teammates all wear disposable overalls, paper shoe covers, **latex** gloves, and some wear face masks. When they leave, the team hands their gloves and paper clothes in as evidence, too. Some important information may have stuck to their clothing.

CRIME SCENE DO NO   ENE DO NOT

face mask

overalls

shoe covers

latex gloves

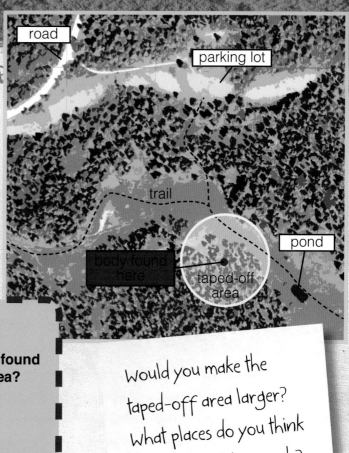

road

parking lot

trail

pond

body found here

taped-off area

Andrea first checks that the taped-off area is large enough. Sometimes, vital evidence may be found far away from the body.

Solve It!

What evidence might be found outside the search area?

a) tire tracks

b) the murder weapon

c) footprints

d) a, b, and c

Answers on page 45

Would you make the taped-off area larger? What places do you think are important to search?

The CSI team starts by doing a walk around, to get a feel for the crime scene. Andrea checks to see if anyone moved anything before her team arrived. She takes note of any potential evidence. The team is careful not to touch anything.

Once all the photographs, videos, and sketches are done, the team does a second walk around the area. They double-check they have recorded everything of interest. The team still touches nothing.

Searching a Crime Scene

Imagine you are leading a CSI team at the crime scene at Tall Trees Trail. You need to organize a search of the area. There are several different search methods that teams use. Which do you think would work best here?

parallel

The search team forms a line side by side and searches the area.

grid

The search team does one parallel search followed by another at right angles.

zone

The area is separated into a grid. Each team member searches a square.

outward spiral

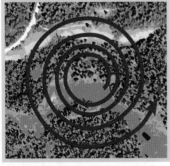

This method works best if there is just one CSI. Spiral out from the center.

inward spiral

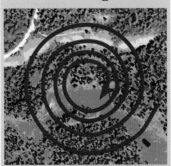

Similar to the outward spiral, except the searcher spirals in from the edge.

wheel

The team starts at the center and searches outward in straight lines.

What are search teams looking for?

- anything out of place
- personal items such as phone, wallets, or keys
- **discarded** clothing
- footprints
- drag marks
- tire marks
- blood
- the murder weapon
- shell casings, if the weapon was a gun
- freshly dug earth

Hunt the Evidence

Get some friends to play this game with you. One of you will hide several pieces of evidence in an outdoor space. The rest of you are the search team. Try the different search methods and see which one works best. Record which method you used and how successful it was.

Search Method	Number of finds
Parallel search	3
Grid	5
Zone	3
Outward spiral	2
Inward spiral	3
Wheel	3

Top Tip

Don't forget to look up! Evidence can be found in trees and bushes as well as on the ground.

The Search

The Strand of Hair

Scouring the crime scene on that bright winter morning, the CSI team found some tiny but important clues. A strand of hair was caught in the knot of the victim's scarf, and another could be seen in a fold of his sweater. Andrea knelt down. She must not touch the hairs. Using tweezers, she carefully places each hair into an envelope.

What secrets can hair hold?

Hair can contain vital evidence. Scientists can work out if a hair came from an animal or a human by looking at the patterns of **cells** and the color of the hair.

In some cases a hair sample can tell whether the person has European, Asian, or African heritage. It can also show if the person was alive or dead when the hair was pulled out.

If **DNA** can be found, examiners can tell if the person was male or female, and even link people with the same mother.

EVIDENCE BAG CHALLENGE

You will need: some tape, a strand of your hair, a strand of a friend's hair, an old wool sweater, some paper, a pen

1. Set a challenge for a friend. Take a strand of your own hair from your hairbrush. Place the strand on a strip of tape. Stick it on the paper and mark it "Sample A."

2. Find someone with straighter, curlier, or different color hair than yours. Mark their strand "Sample B."

3. Pull a strand from an old wool sweater and mark that "Sample C." Challenge your friend to guess where each hair came from. How well did they do?

Sample A

Sample B

Sample C

The **forensic** team back at the **laboratory** knows Andrea wants to help crack this case. They let her come and see the hair samples under their powerful microscopes. Close up, she can still see the root attached to one of the samples. That means the hair may contain vital DNA. The Lab team gets to work analyzing the hair root. They'll let Andrea know what they find. Will it be from the victim – or could it help catch the killer?

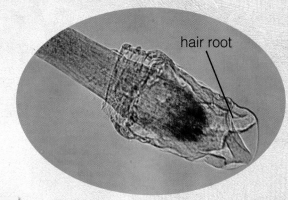

hair root

What Story Can The Victim Tell?

Once the hair samples have been taken, Andrea and her team take another look at the victim. He has what appears to be a gunshot wound in his chest. They take photographs to record the position of the body and any evidence that may be disturbed once the victim is moved. The coroner checks over the body, to see if he can work out the time and cause of death.

The CSI team carefully prepares the victim, so he can be taken away to be properly examined. They tape paper bags over the hands and feet so that no evidence is lost while transporting the body to the coroner's office. Then the body is carefully zipped into a bag and taken away. The team searches the area where the body lay for more clues.

Who does what at a crime scene?

Detectives investigate the crime. They interview witnesses and suspects and try to solve the case.

The CSI team records the crime scene and collects evidence for the forensic experts.

CSI specialists such as **blood spatter analysts** or **ballistic experts** will analyze evidence found by the CSI team back at their laboratories.

Forensics teams examine the evidence, such as hair samples and fingerprints, back at their laboratories.

The coroner or medical examiner examines the victim at the scene, and transports the body for further examination. They, or a **pathologist,** may perform an **autopsy**, which examines the body for more clues as to how the victim died.

Solve It!

Andrea notices there is hardly any blood on the ground once the body is moved. What could that mean?

a) the victim may not have been murdered where he was found

b) the victim may have worn a tight T-shirt

Answers on page 45

Andrea asks herself some questions as the team prepares the body to be taken away. Why is the victim's clothing bunched up? Has the body been dragged? The man has a white mark around his wrist. Could that be a tan mark from where a watch once was? Was he robbed, or did the watch fall off?

SCIENCE DETECTIVE

Protecting Evidence

When the case you have been working on gets to court, there is nothing a **defense attorney** likes better than if vital evidence has been spoiled! It can mean a guilty person goes free. Different types of evidence need to be stored in different ways, and it is a CSI's job to know the right way!

EVIDENCE BAG CHALLENGE

You will need: four grapes, two plastic food bags, a paper bag, a pen and paper

A grape has been found at a crime scene! It may contain poison or other evidence. What would be the best way to store a juicy grape?

1. Place one grape on a plate, another in a paper bag, a third in a plastic bag, and the final grape in a plastic bag placed in the freezer.

2. Try to **predict** which grape will stay the freshest. Write your prediction down.

3. Check on each grape after two days, and then again after a week. Which grapes look old and moldy? Which grapes are still fresh? Was your prediction right? Which method do you think is the best way to store evidence with a liquid content?

Gloves used at the crime scene can become contaminated. It is important to change gloves between handling each item. If you pick up an item at the scene, it may have the suspect's DNA on it. If you touch another item using the same gloves, you could transfer DNA to that, too. Also CSIs must be careful not to touch their own eyes, nose, or mouth with the gloves. If they do, they must change gloves. If a court thinks a CSI's methods have been sloppy, they will not believe any of the evidence is real.

Top Tip

Some CSIs wear one pair of gloves on top of another, for a quick change!

Clean Evidence?

Try this experiment to see if you can keep the evidence clean.

You will need: a bowl of cocoa powder, a bowl of flour, latex or rubber gloves, a sheet of white paper, a magnifying glass

1. Put on the gloves. Dip your fingers in the bowl of cocoa powder. Shake the powder off again over the bowl.

2. Now pinch some flour and place it onto the paper. Can you see any cocoa in the flour? What about if you use a magnifying glass?

Footprints in the mud

How did the victim get to the middle of the forest? Was he murdered here, or was he brought here afterward? The CSI team spreads out and starts to search the area for any drag marks, footprints, or tire marks. They tread carefully. Andrea had already noticed what looked like a large, man's footprint near the body on her walk-through. She had placed a marker beside it.

Footprints can be matched to particular shoes, as even small marks on the soles can leave imprints in the ground. Photographs can record a footprint, but the best way to preserve this type of evidence is to take a plaster impression.

Solve It!

Look at the bottom of some of your shoes. Most soles have very distinct patterns. What type of shoe do you think made this footprint?

a) a ballet flat

b) a workman's boot

c) a basketball shoe

Answers on page 45

How to Make a Print Cast

The CSI team believes that the footprint could belong to the murderer. They decide to make a plaster cast of the print to keep as evidence.

1 Special plastic strips are carefully placed around the footprint. Care is taken to place them far enough away from the print so as not to damage it.

2 A plaster mix is slowly poured into one end of the area. The team gently taps the plaster with a pen to remove any air bubbles.

3 Once the cast is completely dry, it is lifted out of the ground. The team wraps the cast in paper. Back at the lab, a team will gently brush the soil away and store the evidence safely.

Evidence File

Helpful Footprints

Did you know that you can tell a person's approximate height and weight just from studying their footprint? A heavier person will make a deeper print into the soil than a lighter person will. A change in the depth may mean the person's weight has changed. Perhaps they are carrying a heavy object and then putting it down?

Make a Foot Size/Height Scatter Graph

Can you guess someone's height from their footprint? Plot your friends' feet sizes and heights on a scatter graph to find out. Trace the graph below, but without the dots. Place a ruler along your graph at each person's shoe size. Move your finger along the ruler and place a dot when you are directly above their height. You will probably end up with a pattern a little like the one below. What does it tell you?

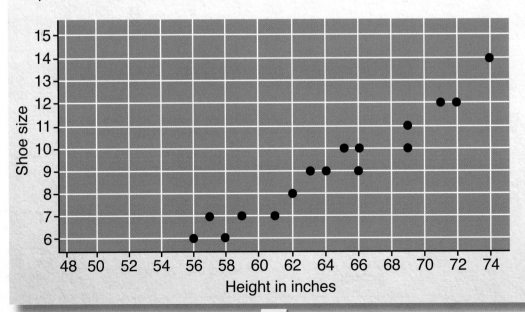

EVIDENCE BAG CHALLENGE

You will need: watercolor paint, a large brush or roller, several sheets of paper, a friend, some sticky notes, a pen

Collect some different shoes. Make sure you ask permission before you borrow anyone else's shoes!

1. Cover an area with newspaper and wear old clothes. Using the roller or brush, paint the bottom of a shoe. Press the shoe onto the white paper. You may want to rock the shoe gently back and forth to get a good print. Lift the shoe straight up from the paper, so the print doesn't smudge. Repeat until you have prints of all the shoes.

2. Label each shoe and the back of each print with a numbered sticky note, so you can remember which is which.

3. Challenge a friend to match the shoe with the print. How well did they do? Don't forget to wash the paint off the shoes once you are done.

Finding Fingerprints

Each person's fingerprints are unique. A fingerprint expert can identify a person who left a print at a crime scene, as long as that person's prints are on file. Andrea looks for any surface that she might be able to check for prints. Indoor crime scenes are much easier. Fingerprints are easiest to find on smooth surfaces. This forest crime scene will be a challenge!

Prints

Fingerprint Types

There are three main types of fingerprints that can be found at a crime scene.

A **Visible** prints. When a person's fingers are covered in blood, wet paint, dirt, or another substance, they may leave a visible print on a surface.

B Impression prints. These are found pressed into soft materials such as putty, chewing gum, or soap.

C Latent prints. These prints are made by the transfer of sweat onto a smooth surface. They are not visible until they are dusted with special powder.

Solve It!

Could you be a fingerprint expert? Try to match the fingerprint found at the crime scene to the correct suspect's print.

a

b

c

d

e

f

Answers on page 45

Andrea finally finds what she has been looking for – a piece of evidence with a nice, smooth surface! Under some leaves, near where the body was found, she finds a wristwatch. The victim's watch had not been stolen after all. Perhaps it fell off while he was being moved? Andrea very carefully bags up the evidence. It is best for the fingerprint experts to check it for prints back at the lab.

SCIENCE DETECTIVE

Dusting for Prints

Imagine someone has been poisoned. A dark glass bottle in your kitchen is the likely murder weapon. Can you work out which of your friends or family members is the killer? You'll need to get some fingerprint evidence, first.

EVIDENCE BAG CHALLENGE

You will need: an ink pad (or makeup sponge, paintbrush, and paint), makeup brush, a dark glass bottle, some white paper, some see-through tape, talcum powder or cornstarch, rubber gloves, hand lotion, a sheet of dark paper

1. Ask your family or friends to choose someone to place their fingerprint on the bottle. They will need to put a little hand lotion on their finger first, to make the print easy to find.

2. Now it's up to you to catch the killer! Take fingerprints from the suspects. Press each finger firmly into the ink pad. Then press each finger onto a sheet of white paper. If you do not have an ink pad, make one by brushing a thick coat of paint on to a dampened makeup sponge. Use a different sheet of white paper for each suspect and write their name at the top.

3. Now that you have your suspects on file, it's time to see who is the culprit. Put on the rubber gloves and handle the bottle carefully so as not to smudge any prints. Lightly dust the talcum powder or cornstarch onto the print. Use a makeup brush to very gently brush away any excess powder. Try not to smudge the print.

4. Take a piece of clean tape and gently place it over the print. Don't press the tape or the print may smudge. Carefully lift the tape and you should be able to see the fingerprint appear on the tape. To see the print more easily, stick the tape onto a sheet of dark paper. Can you find a match?

How do prints occur? Our skin produces oils that get left behind when we touch objects. The powder sticks to the oils and shows up the pattern made by ridges in our skin.

Prints

Arches, Whorls, and Loops

The **FBI** categorizes prints by three main patterns: arches, loops, and whorls.

A   Arches are found in about 5 percent of fingerprint patterns encountered.

B   Loops are the most common type of fingerprint pattern. They occur in about 60-70 percent of fingerprints.

C   Whorls are seen in about 25-35 percent of fingerprint patterns.

Which pattern do you have?

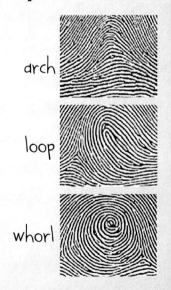

arch

loop

whorl

Hunting Tire Tracks and Drag Marks

Andrea had thought the body looked like it had been dragged. Where could it have been dragged from? It was probably the parking lot, just north of the crime scene. That area will need some special attention. The team spreads out and heads toward the parking lot, hoping to find some drag marks and vehicle tracks.

They quickly pick up what looks like a trail of drag marks. The marks follow an odd path. For a while the marks follow the trail, but then move into the trees. Why?

Top Tip

CSI teams must not assume too much. They need to keep an open mind, in case they miss evidence because they weren't looking for it.

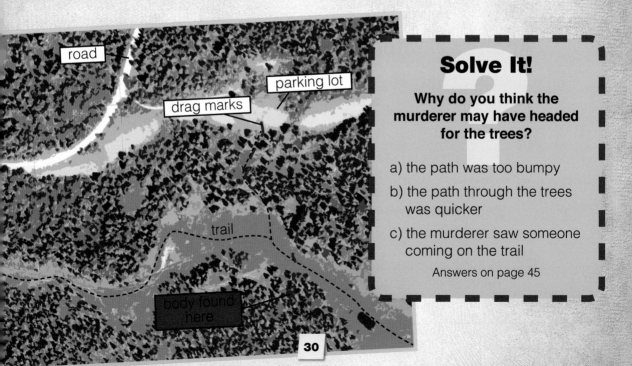

road

parking lot

drag marks

trail

body found here

Solve It!

Why do you think the murderer may have headed for the trees?

a) the path was too bumpy

b) the path through the trees was quicker

c) the murderer saw someone coming on the trail

Answers on page 45

Not surprisingly, at the parking lot, the CSI team finds many sets of tire tracks. Most look as though they were made several days before. There are two sets that look fresh. The team gets to work photographing them, and taking casts.

Specialists can study the tracks and work out the type and brand of tire, and even match it to a vehicle. Uneven wear on tires can mean they leave tracks almost as unique as fingerprints!

Tires

How to Match a Tire Track

Police agencies have **databases** listing all the different types of tires. Investigators can use these databases to narrow in on what type of vehicle left the tracks. The investigator identifies any patterns in the tire print, such as waves, lines, diamonds, zigzags, etc. They select pictures from the database of the patterns that best match their tire mark. Then the database searches for the most likely matches.

Investigators also measure the distance between the front of the tires and rear of the tires on the same side. This can help them work out how long a vehicle is.

Can You Match Tire Tracks?

Bike tires can have several different patterns in their tread, just like car tires. Try to see if you can tell the difference between two bike tire tread prints.

You will need: two bicycles, a large sheet of paper, some kids' paint, a large paintbrush

- Choose two tires that look a little different. Even if the tires have the same pattern they may have different levels of wear. These two tires were on the same bike, but look completely different.

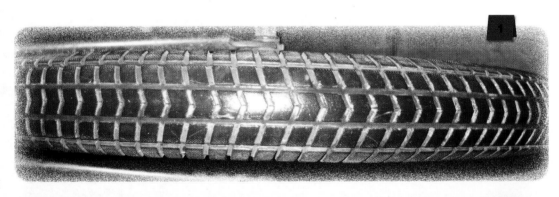

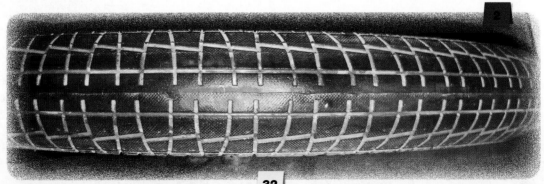

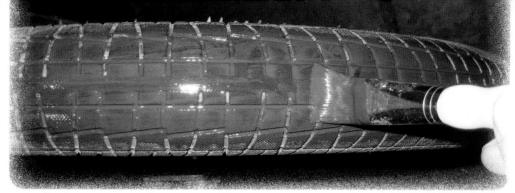

- Using a large brush, paint a section of one of the bike's tires.

- Carefully roll the bike over the paper to make a print. Label the first print "Exhibit A."

- Do the same with the second bike, using the same color, but label this print "Exhibit B."

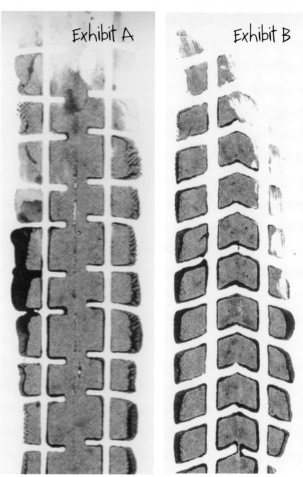

Exhibit A

Exhibit B

Top Tip

It helps if you sit on the bike as you roll it across the paper. Your weight squashes the tire and helps create a wider tire track.

- Examine the tracks. Can you spot any differences? Even identical bikes will usually have slightly different wear on each tire. Can you tell which tire made which track?

The Empty Bottle

While searching the parking lot, Andrea finds a bottle. Evidence like this can be really important. Why? Because investigators may be able to find DNA evidence on it. DNA is a substance found in a body's cells. DNA can be found in saliva, for example, or on the hair root that Andrea found earlier. Body fluids are tested for DNA and the results are matched against police records. When anyone is arrested, their DNA is taken and stored on a police database. Maybe saliva on this bottle could help catch the killer.

Solve It!

Why do you think there is a big and a little number 8 on the crime scene marker?

a) in case one of the numbers rubs off

b) the number is really 88

c) a close-up photograph may not show all of the big number 8

Answers on page 45

How to Match DNA

Each person's DNA has a unique **sequence**. The sequence can be turned into a picture that looks a little like a bar code. If the strips in the DNA code line up exactly, then you have found a match. Which of the three suspects below do you think was at the crime scene?

Answer on p 45

Suspect 1

Suspect 3

DNA found at crime scene

Suspect 2

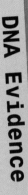

DNA Evidence

Everyone's DNA is different – apart from some identical twins. There are always family similarities, however. If DNA found at a crime scene quite closely matches a sample already on a police database, the police may suspect that it belongs to a relative of that person. The police might bring in family members of the person on their database, until they find an exact match.

DO WE HAVE EVERYTHING?

P robably the most difficult part of Andrea's job is deciding when to "release" the crime scene. She must only release it when the CSI team believes they have all the evidence the crime scene can provide. They then gather up all their equipment and open the area back up to the public. It is a big decision, particularly at an outdoor crime scene like this one. Every twig or leaf could be hiding something!

Andrea has her team do a final survey. Everyone joins together to double-check that they have searched everywhere and recorded everything correctly.

Solve It!

Flimsy crime scene tape doesn't keep people or animals out by itself. What other methods might CSIs use?

a) police officers guard the perimeter

b) officers write down everyone as they enter and leave

c) CSIs tape off a path for everyone entering and leaving to use

d) all of the above

Answers on page 45

As a final check, Andrea asks one of her officers to take some aerial photographs of the scene using a police drone.

The drone can fly up above the trees and may be able to see things not visible from the ground. The team checks over the images as the drone flies around. There doesn't appear to be anything new that they need to investigate. Andrea has a quick discussion with the detective in charge and then makes the decision to release the crime scene. Time to pack up and head back to the office.

EVIDENCE BAG CHALLENGE

Try this challenge to see how an aerial view can help discover new evidence.

You will need: a handful of small stones, ten grains of uncooked rice

1. Scatter the stones outside over a small area. Lie down next to the stones and sprinkle the rice in among them. How many grains can you see?

2. Now stand up. How many more grains can you see now?

Back in the Office

Andrea and her team head back to the office. They need to safely store all the case's evidence away. They also need to file their photographs, sketches, and notes.

Andrea writes up her report. Andrea believes the victim was probably murdered elsewhere and dragged there from the direction of the parking lot. She must carefully state the facts only, though, and be careful to avoid giving opinions. She reports that drag marks appear to be leading toward the victim's body. This is an accurate fact, not an opinion.

tamper-proof tape

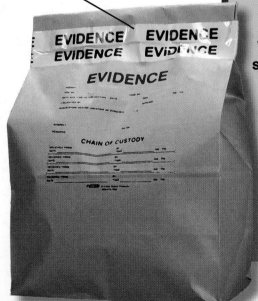

Solve It!

When evidence is stored, every item is secured with tamper-proof tape. What is the main reason for this?

a) to keep dust from getting into the container

b) to make sure no one can open the bag and alter the evidence

c) to prevent evidence from falling out of the container

Answers on page 45

Andrea's notes must be clear, so that anyone else investigating the crime will have a good idea of exactly what she saw that day. One of the ways to do this is by drawing a detailed sketch. A sketch can be more useful than photographs when a crime scene is over a large area, like the one at Tall Trees Trail. A sketch can show the location of important items, and leave out any unimportant details.

EVIDENCE BAG CHALLENGE

You will need: some toys, a stuffed animal, paper, pencil, tape measure, a friend

Create and then sketch your own crime scene.

1 Place your stuffed animal "victim" in the crime scene, and any important evidence around the victim.

2 Draw a sketch of your crime scene. Show any tire tracks, footprints, drag marks, blood, etc.

3 Measure the distances between important objects and add them to your sketch. Ask a friend if they can work out what happened at the scene from your drawing.

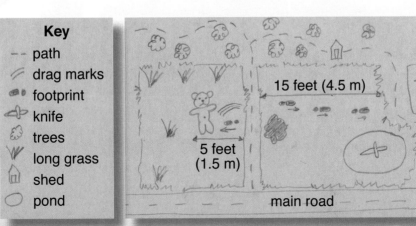

Key
-- path
drag marks
footprint
knife
trees
long grass
shed
pond

15 feet (4.5 m)

5 feet (1.5 m)

parking lot

main road

preparing evidence

Unlike a detective, who may work on one case for some time, CSIs will attend every crime scene in their area. It is not like on a TV show, where CSI teams sometimes solve the crime themselves. Andrea cannot spend too long on one case. She is part of a much larger team, and everyone plays a part in solving the crime. Once the police officers and detectives have interviewed witnesses and suspects, they bring together all the evidence. Only then will someone be charged for the murder in the woods.

CSI Report

Date: Oct 11 2017

Case Number: 0155

Andrea Bray

Tall Trees Trail Murder

Suggestions

- Interview anyone in the parking lot who may have seen suspicious activity
- Interview the jogger that found the body
- Analyze the hair, fingerprint, and saliva for possible DNA or fingerprint matches
- Interview anyone who used the trail in case they saw or heard the killer drag the body off the path

Once a suspect is found

- Check any vehicles to see if their tires match any of the tracks found at the scene
- Search for footwear that might be a match for the footprint found at the scene
- Search vehicles used by the suspect. One may have been used to transport the victim and may have blood or hair evidence.
- See if their DNA or prints match any from the scene

EVIDENCE BAG CHALLENGE

Once detectives have found a suspect and have enough evidence, then there will be a trial. Andrea will be called as a witness. All her precise notes, evidence collection, and storage will be put to the test. How good a witness do you think you would be?

You will need: a pen and paper

1. Cover the upside-down writing at the bottom of this page with a piece of paper. Then, take a look at the photograph for around one minute. Try and notice as much detail as you can.

2. Now cover the photo and see if you can answer questions below.

- How many kids had stars on their T-shirts?
- How many girls had hair in braids?
- How many of the kids' arms were not up in the air?
- What color kite was the boy standing on one leg holding?

A Day in Court

The detectives on the case did great work. Andrea is pleased to hear they have a suspect, and her evidence helped them to find him. DNA samples from the hair strand proved the hair did not come from the victim. By studying its root, forensics specialists could tell that it came from someone of Asian descent. Detectives then had something to go on.

While investigating the victim, detectives found he was Peter Talbot, a blind man who had just arrived in the city on vacation. Witnesses in the neighborhood where he was supposed to be staying said they had heard a gunshot. Detectives began to interview the neighbors.

Solve It!

Peter Talbot had booked a room at a hotel on North Street. He never showed up. John Lee Kim lived next door. Kim's home had been burgled two days earlier. He told friends he was going to get a firearm to protect himself. What do you think might have happened the night Peter Talbot died? The jury will have to decide.

a) Talbot got lost trying to find his hotel room. Kim mistook Talbot for a burglar and shot him. Realizing his mistake, Kim panicked and dumped the body in the woods.

b) Talbot was not really on vacation. He was the burglar who had broken into Kim's home two days ago. To keep Kim from going to the police, Talbot attacked Kim. In the struggle, Kim shot Talbot and then panicked and dumped the body in the woods.

Answers on page 45

Name: John Lee Kim

Date of Trial: 9/17/2018
Court No: Court One

Judge Presiding: D Humboldt

Crime: Murder

Profile: John Lee Kim has no previous criminal record. He worked at the local tattoo parlor. He is described by friends and workmates as friendly and peaceful. He did own a gun. His home had recently been burgled. His car was found burned the day after the murder.

Andrea is called to court to be questioned about the crime scene evidence. To prepare, she looks through her notes and photographs to remind her of the day. The DNA from the bottle matched Kim's DNA. That, and the hair, are vital evidence to prove Kim was at the scene. Shoes matching the footprint were found at his home, with traces of mud that matched the soil at the trail. Andrea calmly gives her evidence, and she's sure she did everything right. Now it's up to the jury to decide. What do you think?

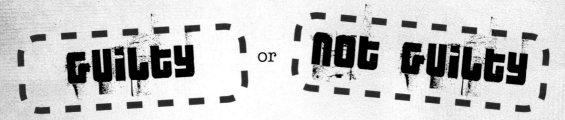

GUILTY or NOT GUILTY

Glossary

autopsy An examination of a dead body especially to find out the cause and manner of death.

ballistic experts Scientists who examine the motion of objects (such as bullets) that are fired.

blood spatter analysts Experts who study and analyze bloodstains at a crime scene to help investigators work out details of the crime.

cells The basic building blocks of all living things, which are continually being renewed.

contaminate Make something impure by adding something undesirable.

coroner An official who holds inquests into violent, sudden, or suspicious deaths.

crime scene The place where an offense has been committed and forensic evidence may be gathered.

databases Collections of data that are organized especially to be used by a computer.

defense attorney A lawyer who represents people facing criminal charges.

discarded To get rid of as useless or unwanted.

DNA The code in each person's cells that makes everyone unique.

evidence Material presented to a court in a crime case.

FBI Federal Bureau of Investigation; an agency of the Justice Department responsible for investigating violations of federal laws.

fibers Threads, or a structure or object resembling threads.

forensic Using scientific methods to investigate and establish facts in criminal courts.

laboratory A place for making scientific experiments, where any forensic evidence is tested.

latex A mixture of water and fine particles of rubber or plastic which can be used to make very thin gloves.

methodical Being in the habit of following a method.

pathologist Forensic scientist who examines samples of body tissue and dead bodies.

predict To decide in advance what will happen based on observation, experience, or reasoning.

sequence The order in which things are or should be connected.

testifying Giving a statement in a legal case.

visible Capable of being seen.

ANSWERS

page 5 - b, page 6 - b, page 13 - d, page 19 - a, page 22 - b, page 27 - e, page 30 - c, page 33 - 1 = Exhibit B, 2= Exhibit A, page 34 - c, page 35 - Suspect 2, page 36 - d, page 38 - b, page 42 - a (Talbot was blind so it is unlikely he was the burglar).

want to be a crime scene investigator?

Job: Crime Scene Investigator

Job Description: CSIs collect and examine evidence at crime scenes. They search for evidence such as fingerprints, hairs, or fibers, to give to a crime lab for analysis. They also photograph the crime scene and take notes of their observations. The job is usually full-time. It may include night or weekend work. CSIs will see some disturbing crime scenes, such as those following violent crimes.

Qualifications needed: A degree in a science subject, criminal justice, or forensic science.

Employment: Many CSIs are police officers first. Once training is complete, officers can apply for CSI jobs within the force. CSIs usually start working for a senior investigator. As they gain more experience, they begin to work on their own cases, with supervision. Once they have done a year working as a CSI, they may take more on-the-job qualifications which can help them get more senior jobs.

Further Qualifications: Many CSIs will take a further degree or take other courses to keep improving their skills.

Career Advice

Further Information

Books

Herwick, Diana. *On the Scene: A CSI's Life*. New York, NY: Time For Kids, 2013.

Gardner, Robert. *Crime Lab 101: 25 Different Experiments in Crime Detection*. Mineola, NY: Dover Publications, 2013.

Websites

Play this cool game to learn about what goes on at a crime scene investigation.
http://kidsahead.com/subjects/10-crime-scene-investigation/activities/600

See if you can solve the crime on this website!
http://www.cyberbee.com/whodunnit/crimescene.html

PUBLISHER'S NOTE TO EDUCATORS AND PARENTS:

Our editors have carefully reviewed these websites to ensure that they are suitable for students. Many websites change frequently, however, and we cannot guarantee that a site's future contents will continue to meet our high standards of quality and educational value. Be advised that students should be closely supervised whenever they access the Internet.

Index